CREATIVE LIVES

Pablo
Picasso

JEREMY WALLIS

Heinemann Library
Chicago, Illinois

Designed by Tinstar
Originated by Ambassador Litho.
Printed and bound in Hong Kong/China

06 05 04 03 02
10 9 8 7 6 5 4 3 2 1

Library of Congress Cataloging-in-Publication Data
Wallis, Jeremy.
  Pablo Picasso / Jeremy Wallis.
     p. cm. -- (Creative lives)
  ISBN 1-58810-206-8
  1. Picasso, Pablo, 1881-1973--Juvenile literature. 2.
Artists--France--Biography--Juvenile literature. [1. Picasso, Pablo,
1881-1973. 2. Artists.] I. Title. II. Series.
  N6853.P5 W338 2001
  709'.2--dc21

                              2001000529

Acknowledgments
The author and publishers are grateful to the following for permission to reproduce
copyright material: pp. 5, 18, 20, 40, 48, 52 Bridgeman Art Library; pp. 7, 10, 25, 43, 51, 55
AKG; p. 12 Museu Picasso, Barcelona; pp. 13, 19, 23, 26, 29, 36 Musée Picasso, Paris; p. 15
Guggenheim Museum, New York; p. 17 J. Faujour; pp. 20, 22 The Metropolitan Museum of
Art; p. 28 Archives de la Fondation Erik Satie; p. 31 Coursaget; pp. 33, 34 J.G. Berizzi; p. 35
The Art Institute of Chicago; p. 39 Michele Bellot; pp. 42, 47 Museum of Modern Art, New
York; p. 44 Beatrice Hatala; p. 49 Courtesy of the Trustees of the V&A; p. 53 Herve
Lewandowski.

Cover photograph reproduced with permission of Hulton Getty.

Every effort has been made to contact copyright holders of any material reproduced in this
book. Any omissions will be rectified in subsequent printings if notice is given to the
publisher.

Some words are shown in bold, **like this.** You can find out what they mean by looking
in the glossary. Some names are shown in bold, **like this.** You can find out who these
people are by looking at pages 58–59.

Contents

Who Was Pablo Picasso?

Pablo Picasso was one of the most famous artists of the twentieth century, and one of the greatest artists of all time. A talented artist, he remade himself many times with consistently new ideas, until the very end of his life, at age 92. The extraordinary events of his life gradually took on a near legendary quality, until Picasso resembled a character from one of the ancient Greek myths he loved so much.

Picasso lived his life publicly. He was the first world-famous artist in the age of celebrity, when the media—newspapers, magazines, newsreels, film, television, and radio—communicated his works, words, and deeds around the world. He took inspiration from wherever he found it: from his Catholic upbringing, African artifacts, the art of the Pacific Islands, the primitive works of his Spanish forebears, the lasting Islamic influence in Spain, his relationships, and important events throughout the world during his lifetime.

By avoiding association with any single style or school of art, Picasso avoided labels. He jumped like a grasshopper from phase to phase. He was always inventing, always making others ask questions and think about new ideas, and he attracted devotion and criticism in equal measure. People who know his work love it or hate it—with Picasso, there is no in-between.

Understanding Picasso

It is important to study Picasso the man—understanding his life and character is important in understanding his art. The reverse is also true —to know the man, it is important to know and understand his art. Each of Picasso's advances in technique, interpretation, and style was accompanied by a large change or movement in his personal life. His happiness or unhappiness in his relationships with others profoundly influenced his work. Every time Picasso broke with his own artistic precedents, he also broke with huge parts of his past life— wives, children, homes, and friends.

In many ways Pablo Picasso remains a mystery. He was a great artist and a man who could be very cruel to his family and friends. It is important to remember that the stories Picasso told about his life are pieces of art created by Picasso. While he was alive, he controlled his public image, and only showed the world one part of his personality.

Picasso painted *Self-Portrait with Coat* in 1901. He was 20 years old, and was becoming a well-known artist.

Picasso's Early Life

On October 25, 1881, Pablo Ruiz y Picasso was born dead in Málaga, Spain. Set aside by the midwife, he was saved by his uncle's quick thinking: leaning over, his uncle Salvador blew a full breath of cigar smoke into the infant's face. The great artist Picasso entered life with a grimace and a shriek of fury. He would later claim his birth was the source of his **hypochondria.**

Pablo's father, José Ruiz Blasco, was a charming dreamer and an artist. He worked as **curator** of the Municipal Museum in Málaga, in the Spanish province of Andalucía. In Maria Picasso López, seventeen years his junior, he found a wife with the steely determination he lacked. They married in December 1880. Within a month, Maria was pregnant with Pablo.

Little Pablo—or "Pablito," as everyone called him—lived in a crowded house with his parents, Maria's unmarried sisters, and her widowed mother. Though not wealthy, it was a respectable, **middle-class,** and cultured household. Everyone fussed over the handsome Pablito. "He was an angel and a devil in beauty," his mother said.

From José, Pablo learned the basics of art. José particularly liked to paint doves and Picasso would claim he always associated them with a childlike sense of peace, innocence, and hope. "There were always doves around … captured in the dining room pictures." Before he could speak, Picasso made his wishes known by drawing, discovering he could earn fried, sugared dough—*churros*—simply by drawing them. His first word was *"Piz!"*—short for *lápiz*, meaning pencil. Picasso also shared his father's passion for the bullfight.

> **"**
> Picasso's mother, Maria Picasso López, once said to him:
> *"If you become a soldier, you will be a general. And if you become a monk, you will be the pope."*
> **"**

Life in Málaga

Picasso spent his early years in Málaga, where a steep rocky hill with an *alcázar,* or castle, at the top dominates the town. In December 1884, Málaga was shaken by an earthquake. José led his pregnant wife and Pablo to a friend's house built into the rock below the castle. There, Maria gave birth to Pablo's sister, Dolores, who would always be known as "Lola." His sister's sudden arrival, in the midst of this storm of dirt and fear, had a profound impact on the little boy: he was no longer the sole object of everyone's attention!

From the castle rock, you can still see the bull ring, the cathedral, and the churches in Málaga. Picasso remembered many scenes from this time in his life: the traditions of Spanish Catholicism, the tortured figure of Christ that adorned the churches, the spectacle of *Semana Santa,* or Easter Holy Week, and the pageantry of the bullfights he enjoyed. These are powerful images that appear in his work throughout his career.

At fifteen, Pablo Picasso was already a skilled artist, but his difficulty with words and numbers made him very unhappy at school.

Early signs of talent

As a child, Pablo cut out the shapes of animals, people, and flowers and projected them onto a wall. In his cousins, he found a good audience: "draw us a dog, a chicken … a donkey!" In 1888, Picasso began to paint under his father's teaching. At the same time his progress in other subjects at school was very poor. By the age of six he hated school so much that a maid had to drag him through the streets and into the classroom.

In 1891, José accepted a teaching post at the School of Fine Arts in Coruña, in the province of Galicia. Pablo seemed to settle well there. With his new friends, he organized mock bullfights and chased the street cats. While Pablo continued to show remarkable talent as an artist, he could not make sense of numbers or words. Instead of numbers he saw shapes: 7 was an upside-down nose, 2 was a woman kneeling in prayer, 4 was a sailboat on the ocean. He could not see them as numbers with a value. It is now thought he had **dyslexia.**

In 1892, Pablo was accepted as a student at the School of Fine Arts, where his father taught. He was only ten years old. His talent was extraordinary, and his subjects were adult: figures from mythology, portraits, and landscapes. "I had never done children's drawings," Picasso later declared. Of an exhibition of children's art, he said, "I could not have taken part. When I was twelve, I was drawing like **Raphael.**"

Defining moments

In 1895, when Pablo was thirteen, his eight-year-old sister, Concepción, whom everyone called Conchita, contracted **diphtheria.** Picasso made a desperate deal with God: he would not paint again if God saved Conchita. When she died, on January 10, Pablo felt terribly guilty. He was torn between wanting his sister saved, but not wanting to surrender his art. Although he was guilt-stricken, Pablo became convinced that Conchita's death represented God's permission for him to dedicate his life to art.

Not long after Conchita's death, Pablo's father asked Pablo to paint some pigeons' feet as part of a picture while he went out. When he returned, Pablo had finished. Don José immediately handed his palette, paints, and brushes to the boy. He would paint no more, he announced, since the son had overtaken the father.

That same year Don José secured a teaching post at the Barcelona School of Fine Arts. He wanted Pablo admitted as a senior student. Candidates had a month to complete the entrance exam. Famously, Picasso claimed he completed it in a day. The works he submitted actually have two separate dates, but this was still a remarkable achievement for a fourteen-year-old artist. The examiners awarded Picasso the highest grade.

Though Picasso claimed the teachers could not teach him anything and that he owed nothing to the **old masters,** the technical training he received gave him a solid foundation for his artistic development. Picasso's rebelliousness was in keeping with the times: the fast-approaching twentieth century stimulated rebellion everywhere.

Spain in turmoil

Throughout Spain in the 1890s, while Pablo was growing up, people demanded change. They believed the **monarchy** and church had failed them and had cheated them. In the countryside, peasants who worked all day for a loaf of bread rose in revolt. In the towns, intellectuals rejected the old political, cultural, and artistic traditions and working people demanded rights and freedoms. **Socialism,** powerful outside Spain, grew in influence, and **Anarchism** was more powerful here than anywhere else. In provinces such as Cataluña and the Basque region, many saw themselves as a separate people, and demanded independence.

Throughout Spain, people looked at the economic, social, and political progress made in France, Britain, Germany, and the U.S., and were desperate to drag Spain into the twentieth century. Many artists sympathized with this.

Growing up and moving on

Picasso persuaded his father to set him up in his own studio, where he painted *Science and Charity*. The writer Denis Thomas called it the "last work of his boyhood, and … the first … of his manhood." Picasso composed many pictures on religious themes. He rejected organized religion, but Picasso often used Christ's tortured figure as a symbol of suffering.

Many of his paintings at this time were reproductions of other artists' work—especially of the French artist **Toulouse-Lautrec** and the English Pre-Raphaelite Brotherhood. However, he knew little of the **Impressionists,** a group of artists who were working in France.

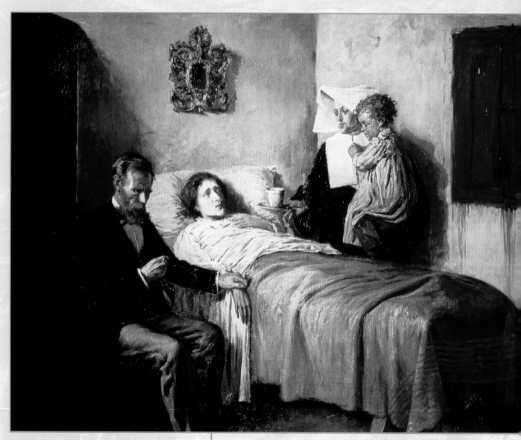

Pablo's father modeled as the doctor in *Science and Charity*, 1897. The painting won an award at an art exhibition in Madrid, before being given to Pablo's uncle, Don Salvador.

The Pre-Raphaelite Brotherhood

The Pre-Raphaelite Brotherhood was a group of artists who formed in London in 1848. Their intention was to revolutionize modern art and reinvent painting in the style of fifteenth-century Italian artists—that is, painters who worked before the Italian painter **Raphael.** They wanted to paint serious subjects and to study nature closely. They avoided heavy shadows in their work and rejected the dark and nondetailed style of other artists working at the time. Instead, they painted with bright colors on a white background. They became known for their hard-edged forms, their realism, and their attention to detail.

At this time, Pablo's attitude toward his father changed. Don José nurtured his son's talent, but Pablo resented his father's constructive criticism and advice. He preferred his mother's unthinking and absolute adoration of his charm and abilities. He took Picasso, her family name, as his own last name. When Pablo enrolled at the Royal Academy in Madrid in 1897, at the age of sixteen, he denied his father's role as his teacher. He completed his entrance tests in a day. His extended family pooled their resources to pay for his studies.

While in Madrid, Picasso visited the national collection of art at the Prado Museum. This opened his eyes to the work of the **old masters,** such as **El Greco.** However, the Academy disappointed him: he found the style of instruction boring. Instead, he preferred to roam the streets and squares or spend his time in bars and cafes watching people. A tutor at the Royal Academy, who was also a friend of his father, reported Pablo's skipped classes, lack of work, and poor attitude. His relatives cut his allowance off. Only his father continued to send money. Too poor even to rent a studio, Pablo was reduced to painting in the open air. In the spring of 1898, illness provided the excuse he needed to leave.

Illness and recovery

A painter friend, Manuel Pallarés, invited Pablo to recuperate in his village in the Catalán mountains. Picasso would stay there for six months. Creating stories about his past, Picasso later described the village as a lost paradise: "All I know I learned in the village where Pallarés was born."

Manuel and Pablo traveled into the mountains, with a young gypsy guide, to paint. Picasso later claimed that the gypsy taught him the meaning of the birds' songs, the names of the trees, and the movements of the stars. Picasso fell in love with the freedom of gypsy culture. Years later a poet said, "In the great nation of the gypsies of art, Picasso is the most gypsy of all." Picasso enjoyed this remark.

Self-Portrait, 1899–1900, was painted when Picasso was only 18 years old. Picasso was already confident of his artistic ability.

When Picasso returned to Barcelona in 1899, he realized things had changed. Spain was struggling to define itself after losing the Spanish American War. The war, fought between Spain and the U.S., had resulted in the former Spanish colony Cuba winning independence from Spain. Three other Spanish colonies, Puerto Rico, Guam, and the Philippines, now belonged to the U.S. Without the money coming in from the colonies, Spain fell into a depression. People lost their jobs, disabled soldiers begged in the streets, and people demanded change. Picasso's work gradually became darker.

Artists, **Anarchists, Modernists,** and Catalán **Nationalists** met and held exhibitions and performances in a bar called *Els Quatre Gats*— "The Four Cats." Picasso was involved in these gatherings, and he became part of a group of young artists and poets. Picasso was only 19 years old, but he joined in the political arguments with confidence.

In 1900, Picasso held his first one-man show at *Els Quatre Gats*. Around this time he met the poet Jaime Sabartés. Pablo introduced himself as Pablo Ruiz Picasso. Sabartés called him "Picasso"—a single name that seemed to suit him best. Sabartés later said "we spoke of him as of a legendary hero." Sabartés would later add to and pass on the Picasso myth.

In 1899, Picasso designed this illustration for the menu at *Els Quatre Gats*. The bar was a center for ferocious political debates, and Picasso's closest friends were people he met there.

13

The Blue Period

In October 1900, just before his nineteenth birthday, Picasso made his first visit to Paris. He made the journey with a close friend from *Els Quatre Gats,* a fellow artist named Carlos Casagemas. In preparation for their journey, the friends had identical suits made in black corduroy. Broad, muscular, and barrel-chested, Picasso was proud, vain, and confident of his physical power. He spoke no French and had no place to stay, but other Spanish people living in Paris helped him find a place to live and a studio. One of these people, a Catalán businessman named Petrus Mañach, was so impressed with the dynamic young artist that he agreed to pay Picasso 150 francs a month for his entire output.

Picasso toured art galleries, studying the **Impressionists** and the artist **Delacroix,** painters who painted the world around them with bright colors. Visiting theaters and music halls, Picasso fell in love with the poor but colorful entertainers' world, and with the entertainers' freedom from responsibility.

Picasso's stay was cut short when he agreed to take Casagemas home to Málaga for Christmas, to help him recover from an unhappy love affair. Picasso's family was displeased with his wild appearance, so he left for Madrid. Casagemas returned to Paris and shot himself. The shock of her son's death gave Casagemas's mother a heart attack, which killed her. In Picasso—according to one biographer—Casagemas's death created sorrow, guilt, and rage. Picasso returned to Paris, and took over his dead friend's studio.

The suicide of Casagemas

Art became a means for Picasso to come to terms with his experiences. When Casagemas died, he responded to his friend's death by working extremely hard on his art. Picasso's *Evocation (The Burial of Casagemas)* was full of **symbolism.** *Evocation* marked the beginning of Picasso's Blue Period, in which he used dark colors to paint poor, depressed people. These paintings reflected Picasso's feelings at the time.

The Impressionists

Today, the works of **Monet, Renoir, Pissarro, Degas,** and **Manet** are among the most recognized in the world. The Impressionists painted quickly, to recreate the effect of light on objects, and to capture a moment in time like a photograph. Previous generations of artists had portrayed the rich and religious, but the Impressionists recorded the lives of ordinary working people. Impressionism was the first movement of **Modernism,** and led to almost every major artistic movement of the twentieth century.

France became the center of Modernism in literature, drama, and sculpture, as well as painting.

After the death of Casagemas, Picasso filled his paintings with people on the fringes of society. In *Woman Ironing*, painted in 1904, Picasso captured the physical difficulty of modern labor. Picasso wanted to show that the hard work society expected of this woman is hard on her body.

15

> " Many years after Casagemas's death, Picasso took a companion, Françoise Gilot, to a dirty Paris apartment. He wanted to show her that nothing, not even great beauty, lasts forever. In the apartment a toothless old woman was dying. Picasso said: *"When she was young she was very pretty and made a painter friend of mine suffer so much he committed suicide … She turned a lot of heads. Now look at her."* "

Depression in Paris

From this time, Picasso was obsessed by grief and a sense of **exile** from Spain. His isolation was emphasized by the fact that he did not speak French at the time and relied on a small group of Spanish-speaking friends. In his work he expressed his solitude in blue tones. His subjects were victims, trampled by circumstances.

There were other pressures on him, too. He found Parisian winters oppressive, and his relationship with Mañach, who was still buying all his work, worsened. There was no demand for depressing images of suffering and Mañach could not sell Picasso's pictures—but Picasso would not compromise and paint more marketable images. Picasso's depression deepened. In 1902, he turned his back on his growing reputation as an artist in Paris and begged the train fare back to Barcelona from his father. However, his dependency on others, especially his father, made Picasso's depression worse.

Paris again

In 1904, Picasso returned to and finally settled in Paris. He moved into a run-down building in the artists' district of Montmartre. His neighbors—artists, writers, musicians, down-and-outs, crooks—provided Picasso with models for his blue themes. Even so, he never went out alone after dark.

In August, Picasso met a beautiful, intelligent young woman named Fernande Olivier. Later she described him as "small, black, thickset … with piercing black eyes." They became companions, and with Fernande, Picasso found the calm he needed to break his blue mood.

The building where he lived, nicknamed the *Bateau Lavoir*—Laundry Boat—became a magnet for a circle of brilliant friends: the famous painters **Henri Matisse, Georges Braque,** and **Marie Laurencin,** the poets **Max Jacob** and **Guillaume Apollinaire,** and the rich American **bohemians** Leo and **Gertrude Stein.** Picasso put up a sign, "The Poets' Rendezvous." Max Jacob later called the time he spent with this group "the most wonderful days of my life." Picasso also remembered his time with this group as the best time of his life.

Picasso posed for this photo in Montmartre, in 1904. A seedy part of Paris, Montmartre soon became famous for its artistic residents.

The Rose Period

At age 24, Picasso was more confident, and was secure in his relationship with Fernande. The depressing blue tones were replaced and a warmer, more lively rose color began to dominate his work. Picasso's choice of colors now included pinks, ivory white, and muted greens, blues, and yellows.

Picasso visited the nearby *Circus Médrano* up to three times a week. He took the circus performers as his subjects—misfits who seemed to belong everywhere and nowhere. Picasso believed artists and actors were similar because they both created illusions with which to enchant or provoke their audiences. His work also revealed an interest in human relationships, especially between people trapped in their predictable personalities.

Picasso closely identified himself with the character of Harlequin, an unsmiling jester. The melancholy figures of the Rose Period paintings enjoy close relationships and a desire to protect each other from the outside world. Like Harlequin, Picasso saw himself as a tragic misfit, or outsider. He showed Harlequin as a clown who knew how to make other people happy, but did not understand how to be happy himself. Picasso frequently felt the same way.

Picasso often showed Harlequin standing alone. In *Family of Acrobats with an Ape* (1905), Harlequin sits next to a young mother, his stillness in stark contrast to the squirming infant on her lap.

The Rose Period proved popular with critics and buyers alike. In April 1906,

Ambroise Vollard, an important art dealer, bought 30 of Picasso's paintings for 2,000 francs—enough to cover Picasso's household expenses for three years.

A visit to Spain

Pablo and Fernande set out for Spain. She later recalled, "The Picasso I saw in Spain was … less wild, more brilliant and lively … at ease, in fact." After visiting his family and showing Fernande off to his friends, the pair made their way to the village of Gosol, in the Pyrenees Mountains. Gosol was close to the border between Spain and France, and many villagers made a living smuggling. Picasso and Fernande spent days walking in the mountains and nights listening to the smugglers' tales.

This photograph of Picasso with Fernande Olivier was taken in 1906. Fernande gave Picasso the stability he needed to end his Blue Period and develop a new artistic vision.

In Gosol, Picasso developed his interest in **classical** themes. In his Mediterranean phase, Picasso painted Fernande again and again, in a style inspired by ancient Greek art. He was also developing an interest in **primitive art,** stimulated by recently unearthed prehistoric Spanish sculptures he had seen in the Trocadéro and Louvre museums in Paris. New ideas gathered together in his mind and inspired a period of intense creativity. As soon as he and Fernande returned to Paris, Picasso threw himself into painting, inspired by his Spanish travels and the prehistoric art he had seen in Paris. Picasso was about to make his most significant artistic innovation—one that would shake the foundations of European art.

A New Language of Painting

During Picasso's Rose Period, two works stand out in style and painting method—*Portrait of Gertrude Stein* and *Self-Portrait with Palette*. Both paintings demonstrated Picasso's growing interest in the **primitive art** of Africa, Cataluña, and the Pacific, and indicated the direction he was about to take.

Self-Portrait with Palette, 1906, and the *Portrait of Gertrude Stein* are powerful clues to the direction in which Picasso's art was now heading.

Stein's masklike face in *Portrait of Gertrude Stein*, 1906, owed much to the ancient religious masks and artifacts Picasso had been studying.

The portrait of Gertrude Stein

Picasso began his portrait of **Stein** in 1905. He was usually a quick and prolific painter, able to complete a portrait in just one or a few sittings. As the work proceeded, however, Picasso grew increasingly unhappy. In May 1906, after more than 80 sittings, he suddenly painted out the whole head. "I can't see you any longer when I look," he exclaimed. His difficulties were part of a growing sense of frustration with the way his paintings could not express what he wanted them to.

After his trip to Spain with Fernande, energized by the "good air, good water, good milk, and good meat" of Gosol, Picasso completed the portrait—without Stein there. The face was masklike. When people complained Stein did not look like her portrait, Picasso replied, "She will!" Gertrude Stein herself was delighted with it. And just as Picasso predicted, she began to resemble her portrait as she grew older.

Primitive influences

By 1906, a number of artists were being inspired by artifacts such as masks and primitive statues taken from Africa, Latin America, and the Pacific Islands. These were highly simplified, but still very expressive. The French artist **Henri Matisse** wrote of some African statues, "I was struck by their character, their purity of line. It was as fine as Egyptian art. So I bought one … Picasso took to it immediately."

Shock of the new

Picasso was fascinated by these artifacts and began sketches for a painting called *Les Demoiselles d'Avignon*. He completed this painting in 1907, and it marked a great leap forward in his art. The large image he painted of five women shows them with jagged and angular bodies and masklike faces. The picture is groundbreaking because of the way that Picasso distorted his subjects. He was painting the women's bodies from impossible perspectives, and he did not make the picture look like it had three dimensions.

Picasso showed *Les Demoiselles d'Avignon* to his friends. "It's a hoax!" Matisse declared. **André Derain** thought he was having a mental breakdown: "Picasso will be found hanging behind his big picture." **Georges Braque** was shocked and excited: "It is as if Picasso was drinking gasoline and is spitting fire!"

Picasso believed the painting had its own significance. He thought of it as an act of destruction rather than a piece of art. Since the Renaissance, painters had painted people and objects to look like they had three dimensions. Picasso had decided that since a painting only

The painting *Les Demoiselles d'Avignon* (1907) is fragmented into geometric shapes. Picasso worked on it for nine months, and over 800 preparatory sketches survive.

had only two dimensions, an artist did not have to paint a picture to look like it had three dimensions. It could be painted to look like it only had two dimensions, or it could show things in three dimensions from more than one point of view. When Picasso was done with *Les Demoiselles d'Avignon* he rolled the canvas up and put it away for nine years. The painting's reputation had a mysterious power over the art world, even though few people had seen it.

Cubism

By 1907, Picasso and his new painter friend **Braque** were struggling, in Braque's words, like "two mountaineers roped together," to find what Picasso described as "a new language of painting": one that could show four dimensions, including the passage of time, in a two-dimensional art form. They thought painting this way was more honest and realistic. Braque explained, "Imagine a man who would spend his life drawing profiles, as if he would have us believe that Man has only one eye."

It was Braque who first developed the ideas that would be called **Cubism,** and Picasso responded to them. Though about to launch an artistic revolution, they did not name it

This photo of Georges Braque (right) and Fernande Olivier was taken by Picasso. Picasso once compared his partnership with Braque to the partnership of the Wright brothers, who invented the airplane. He even called Braque "Wilbur" after one of the Wright brothers.

themselves. "Cubism" was a derogatory name coined by a critic. Cubism owed much to the French painter **Paul Cézanne,** who believed "everything in nature is modeled on the sphere, the cylinder, and the cone."

Inspired by Braque's Cubist landscapes of L'Estaque, in the south of France, Picasso spent the summer at Horta del Ebro, in Spain, where he completed a series of his own Cubist landscapes. By 1910, Picasso saw himself as a revolutionary. He claimed he was determined to reach the widest audience with his art—even humble peasants and ordinary workers. Despite these claims, he was an **elitist.** He was secretive and enjoyed a childish social life, using a secret language to elevate his circle of friends from the masses.

Picasso liked to promote himself and his art, and many other people were happy to go along with him.

In 1911, Fernande and Pablo spent the summer at Céret, a former monastery in the Pyrenees Mountains. **Braque** joined them. Working together in a studio, Braque and Picasso produced an enormous amount of creative work. They introduced stenciling, song lyrics, shreds of advertising posters, and newspaper headlines into their work. Critics were outraged; one confessed he stood in awe of Picasso, but did not understand what he was looking at.

Changes at home

When Fernande met and fell in love with a young Italian painter, Picasso first showed his strange domestic priorities. He wrote to Braque: "Fernande left yesterday with a … painter. What will I do about the dog?" Within a day Picasso had replaced Fernande. He lured his new girlfriend, Marcelle Humbert, away from his good friend Louis Markus. Marcelle and Pablo fled to Céret, where Picasso renamed her Eva. Later they rented a house near Avignon. Picasso celebrated their love in works like *Jolie Eva*, *Pablo-Eva,* and *Ma Jolie*. He even painted a **still life** on the wall of their house. Picasso's reputation was growing and he knew his work was beginning to command good prices from art collectors. He dismantled the wall and sent it to his Paris art dealer.

During this creative period Picasso began to make sculpture. After seeing paper constructions by Braque, Picasso sculpted *Guitar* from sheet metal and wire. When a critic asked: "What is it?" Picasso replied: "I call it a guitar." Picasso seemed to go from strength to strength. By 1913, he was using vivid color in a development called **Synthetic Cubism.** Over the next few months, Braque began to use collage—art that incorporates paper, cloth, and string with painting. Picasso responded, using, among other things, sand, wood, and cardboard in his next pieces. These were things that he said represented the "waste products of human life." Collage is a common artistic technique today, but in 1913 it was an adventurous and controversial method of creating art.

A changing world

In May, Picasso's father died. Depressed, Picasso spent more time in Céret with Eva. Eva became ill, and doctors diagnosed bronchitis—a serious condition at that time. In September, the couple moved to Paris. The view from their apartment, which looked over a large Paris cemetery, added to Picasso's depression.

In 1914, Picasso's work was exhibited in Europe and in the United States. A German collector bought Picasso's *Saltimbanques*, which had sold for 1,000 francs in 1908, for 11,500 francs, equivalent to tens of thousands of dollars in today's money. This proof of Picasso's popularity provoked outrage in the popular press, which hated his art.

By 1914, Picasso's reputation had grown beyond the Paris art world. But that world was about to be blown apart.

Ma Jolie (1914) refers to Eva Humbert. Picasso never painted a portrait of her. Instead, in honor of Eva, he included the phrase, *ma jolie,* which means "my pretty," in many of his Cubist works.

World War I

For years, competition between the empires of France, Britain, Russia, Germany, and Austria-Hungary had been growing. In June 1914, Serbian **Nationalists** assassinated the heir to the Austrian throne. Austria-Hungary declared war on Serbia. Serbia appealed to Russia for protection. In support of Austria-Hungary, Germany declared war on Russia and its ally France. Germany hoped Britain would remain neutral, but when German troops attacked France through Belgium on August 4, 1914, Britain also declared war on Germany and Austria-Hungary.

Even the forward-thinking European **avant-garde** did not anticipate the horror of World War I. The war changed life in Europe forever. By 1918, over 10 million people were dead, and over 20 million were injured. The war shattered traditional behavior and habits, and brought about new ways of thinking about politics, society, and the arts.

Many French artists, including **Apollinaire, Braque,** and **Derain,** decided to enlist in the army during the war. Picasso saw them off at the station. Braque and Apollinaire both suffered serious head injuries and all three men returned irreversibly altered by their experiences. "I never found them again," Picasso later wrote.

Death of Eva

As a Spanish citizen, Picasso was not required to do military service. Some thought it wrong

Eva Humbert posed for this photo in 1912. She was seriously ill, but she kept the truth from Picasso for fear that he might abandon her.

that he should avoid it, but friends believed his delicate health excused him. Eva's health, which had never been good, got worse. When she finally revealed she had **tuberculosis,** Picasso, the **hypochondriac,** fled in fear to his old studio in the *Bateau Lavoir*. When Eva died, on December 14, 1915, Picasso's art dealer, Daniel-Henry Kahnweiler, blamed him for speeding up her death by exposing her to the intensity of his life and then abandoning her when she needed his help.

By Christmas, Picasso was terribly depressed. He moved home and was burglarized: it probably hurt more that the thieves ignored his paintings and stole only his linen. The only brightness in his life at this time was meeting the poet **Jean Cocteau,** and **Serge Diaghilev,** the director of the famous Russian dance group, the Ballets Russes.

New collaborations

In 1916, Cocteau asked Picasso to design sets and costumes for *Parade*, a ballet created by Cocteau and performed by Diaghilev's Ballets Russes. His designs were a shocking departure from traditional sets, and were typical of Picasso, who believed rules were made to be broken. Apollinaire was also eager to join in. The involvement of so many brilliant but fiercely self-centered artists meant the creative process was regularly disrupted by arguments and fights. *Parade* was almost never made.

Parade

In many ways, *Parade*—based on a fantastically imagined circus —was the first piece of modern performance art. Erik Satie composed music using typewriters and sirens. While some of the crowd cheered for Cocteau, Picasso, Satie, and the performers, others booed. Fights broke out. Only Apollinaire, in uniform and with his head bandaged, prevented a riot. Apollinaire later described *Parade* as **Surrealism.** Picasso was labeled "a dabbler" by critics: they did not believe a serious artist would design sets and costumes for a ballet.

This is one of Picasso's costume designs for the ballet *Parade*, in 1917. It was a radical departure for an artist of Picasso's stature to be designing for the stage.

Olga Koklova

In February 1917, Picasso met Olga Koklova, a dancer with the Ballets Russes who was the daughter of an Imperial Russian General. Olga appealed to Picasso's fascination with Russia, and he thought she was as mysterious as Russia was. Olga's attraction to Picasso appears to have been less complex—he had status, fame, and wealth.

Picasso also met the controversial Russian composer Igor Stravinsky, an artist as revolutionary as he was. In 1913, Stravinsky's ballet *The Rite of Spring* had been so controversial that the dancers were booed and hissed, and his opponents and supporters had fought in the aisles.

In July 1918, Picasso and Olga married and moved into a large, new apartment. Picasso's friends had attended the wedding—with **Max Jacob** and **Apollinaire** playing ceremonial roles—but Olga made it clear that they were no longer welcome in her home.

Seemingly exhausted by his efforts to push back artistic boundaries, Picasso, the most revolutionary artist of the age, sought peace and respect. The **Cubist** painter **Juan Gris,** whom Picasso had criticized in the past, wrote to Kahnweiler: "Picasso still does good things, when he finds time between a Russian ballet and a society portrait."

Picasso tamed?

Picasso seemed like a tame, shackled bull. He presented the wife of his new dealer, Paul Rosenburg, with a painting of her and her son—and she said she would rather have one by Boldini, a fashionable portraitist. In silence, Picasso painted a second picture in the style she wanted, and signed it Boldini.

On November 9, 1918, just before the end of the war, Apollinaire died in the influenza epidemic sweeping the globe. For Picasso, his death was a shock. In many ways it symbolized the end of Picasso's old world. The end of the war, on November 11, represented the birth of the new.

Olga Koklova imposed new conventions on Picasso. When he painted her she said, "I want to recognize my face!"

A New Life

" "It's not what an artist does that counts," Picasso said, "but what he is." "

When the war ended, France was in ruins. War debts were high, and one and a half million Frenchmen were dead. Paris was a shabby, melancholy town. But the city soon revived: as the **Jazz Age** dawned, Paris again became dominant in art and culture. **Gertrude Stein** said Paris is "where the twentieth century is." The celebrity of artists became as important as their art. Picasso and Olga were now caught up in a glittering social life.

When Olga banished art from their apartment, Picasso rented another on the next floor of their building, and turned it into a studio and store. It was soon full of paintings, African masks, ancient artifacts, and books—the accumulation of his life before Olga.

Living the high life

Derain and **Braque** raged against Picasso's surrender to the high life. In response, Picasso called Braque "Madame Picasso," claiming his criticisms were like those of a wife, and belittled both Braque's work and his contribution to **Cubism.**

In contrast to *Parade*, Picasso's next ballet commission, *The Three-Cornered Hat*, was a triumph. Picasso radiated self-confidence: he dressed and lived well, and the public acclaimed his work simply because *he* had painted it, silencing critics who disagreed. The celebrated figure of **Jean Cocteau** led Picasso through the society parties and Picasso's name was featured on every fashionable guest list. Misia Sert, a brilliant hostess who pulled together the circles of high art and high society, invited him to all of her parties. Picasso had decided to sell his art through the dealer Paul Rosenburg, who attracted a "better"—richer—clientele. However, with his new society contacts, it was Picasso, rather than any art dealers, who was in charge of the sale of his canvases and the prices he would charge.

Picasso also worked on a third ballet, Stravinsky's *Pulcinella*. Despite Picasso's long arguments with **Diaghilev,** the ballet and Picasso's contribution won critical praise.

Olga, Picasso, and Jean Cocteau were photographed together in 1917. Picasso and Cocteau were popular guests at fashionable parties.

Fatherhood

In 1920, Picasso and Olga left Paris for Juan-les-Pins, a fashionable resort on the Mediterranean coast. Olga was now pregnant.

It was in Juan-les-Pins that Picasso developed his Neoclassical Style. This was based on the human figure, on the art of the high **Renaissance,** and on his growing fascination with ancient Roman and Greek art. This interest had first developed when, while designing *Parade* in 1917, Picasso traveled to Italy and visited many of the sites of **classical** antiquity, including Rome, Naples, and the buried city of Pompeii. Observing the monumental statues of both Rome and the Renaissance, Picasso was fascinated by their solidity and by the heavy folds of their garments, and he tried to capture this effect in his paintings. Picasso's Neoclassical Style was also inspired by his lasting interest in mythology and the Mediterranean environment around him. The women in his paintings were massive and solid; their faces were impassive masks.

In February 1921, Olga gave birth to a son. Though Picasso was almost 40 years old, Paulo was his first child. Picasso recorded his delight in a series of sketches and paintings. However, he increasingly portrayed mother and son as occupying a self-contained world. Revisiting the themes of the Rose Period, Picasso was once more the distant observer, this time of the close bond between mother and child.

In May, Picasso worked on a fourth ballet, *Cuadro Flamenco*, largely to step in for **Juan Gris.** Gris had been invited to do it originally, but he became ill, which made him late with his designs. The *Cuadro Flamenco* designs did nothing to enhance Picasso's reputation. Many of his old friends, including Gris and Kahnweiler, felt alienated. **Max Jacob** fumed "[Picasso] is deader than **Apollinaire.**" However, there were many who were eager to praise Picasso.

A new style

While Picasso enjoyed the pleasures of fame and the acclaim of high society, his art did not stand still. A new artistic movement called **Surrealism** had emerged. Picasso was the surrealists' hero, because they thought of him as the first artist to liberate his images from the rules and conventions of popular art. Ironically, they were praising him at a time when he was at his most traditional, continuing to explore **classical** themes and fascinated by his infant son.

In 1922, **Jean Cocteau** asked Picasso to design the sets for his version of *Antigone* by Sophocles. The fashion designer **Coco Chanel** was creating the costumes.

Picasso produced his set two days before the premiere. Using chalk on a huge sheet of crumpled canvas, inspired with classical themes, he created a cave of marble, with three columns. Those watching him work burst into applause. *Antigone* was a triumph—though it was Chanel who stole the headlines.

Both Picasso and Chanel were fascinated by each other. She said of his dark, darting eyes: "He is like a sparrow hawk." He admired her rise from poverty in the rural Auvergne region of France to wealth in the height of Parisian society.

Surrealism

Surrealism was an art movement that tried to challenge realism in art and literature by using humor, dream images, and "counter-logic," or the absurd. Most Surrealist art attempted to recreate the world of dreams and the **subconscious.**

After the birth of his first child, Picasso completed many pictures of him, including *Paulo Drawing*, 1923. These pictures belonged to Picasso's personal life and he refused to sell them.

Through 1923 Picasso continued to be celebrated. His name was associated with the explosion of wealth, energy, creativity, and industry that became known as the **Jazz Age.** Meanwhile, his family situation lent him an air of domestic bliss. Critics praised the delicate portraits of his infant while Olga's cool, classic beauty lent itself to Picasso's artistic preoccupations. He immortalized her in a much admired series of paintings and drawings.

Despite Picasso's success, wealth, and the appearance of a happy family life, there were cracks beneath the surface.

33

The End of a Marriage

Picasso was now 42 years old and nearing the height of his fame. But he seemed increasingly unhappy with his new lifestyle and with Olga's social values. The more obvious his unhappiness with the present, the more violently Olga tried to erase his past. At one point she destroyed his old letters from friends that mentioned Fernande. As Picasso withdrew into his imagination, her anger grew.

Picasso's own rage found many targets. When he learned that **Matisse** was designing for the Ballets Russes he raged: "Matisse! What is a Matisse?" Inspired by the **Surrealist** painter **André Breton** and by the young Spanish Surrealist **Joan Miró,** a spiky quality entered Picasso's work. *The Three Dancers*, painted in 1925, was as important a change in his painting style as *Les Demoiselles d'Avignon*

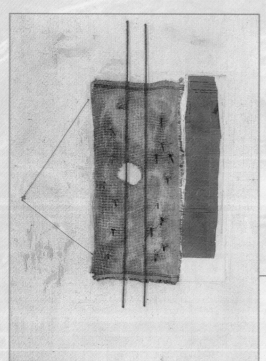

had been. The painting was inspired by the death of Picasso's friend Ramon Pichot. He believed that Pichot's health had been destroyed by his love for the same woman who had driven Casagemas to suicide.

At work and play

In 1925, *Les Demoiselles d'Avignon*, originally completed in 1907, was reproduced for the first time in a publication called *The Surrealist*

In 1925, the Surrealist artist André Breton proclaimed Picasso as "one of us." *Guitar* (1926) was one of several pieces Picasso produced during his Surrealist period.

" *"Give up your easy way of life. Take to the roads."*
André Breton, a Surrealist artist, gave this advice to Picasso in 1925.

Revolution! Picasso joined the first Surrealist exhibition that same year. In 1926 he produced a piece called *Guitar*, this time a collage that included nails hammered out through the canvas. He also planned to mount razor blades and create a work of art that drew blood when it was touched. Though celebrated and inspired by the surrealists, Picasso kept his distance. He realized his artistic freedom depended on not being labeled as a particular type of artist.

In January 1927, Picasso was wandering the streets of Paris, searching for new artistic inspiration using **automatism**—a Surrealist technique to tap into the unconscious mind. Outside the Louvre Museum he met a young woman named Marie-Thérèse Walter. She was seventeen years old. Struck by her beauty and strong athletic posture, Picasso persuaded her to model for him, and he quickly fell in love with her. Love again stirred his imagination: he filled his work with images based on Marie-Thérèse.

In May, **Juan Gris** died. The third member of the **Cubist** partnership, who had inspired the vibrant colors of **Synthetic Cubism,** Gris was just 40 years old. Picasso had cruelly criticized Gris and his work, and had belittled his career, but with characteristic **hypocrisy,** he made sure he was noticed at the funeral. He wanted the public to think of him as a good friend.

The Red Armchair (1931) featured Marie-Thérèse Walter. Noticing her outside the Louvre Museum, Picasso exclaimed: "My name is Picasso—I would like to paint you!"

In July, Picasso, Olga, Paulo, and a nanny left to spend their annual summer vacation at a beach town on the south coast of France. A chauffeur drove them everywhere; "Driving is bad for a painter's wrists,"Picasso claimed, intending a sneer at **Braque,** who loved to drive racing cars. Picasso secretly rented Marie-Thérèse a house nearby.

Picasso's relationship with Marie-Thérèse upset many people—she was very young while he was middle-aged and married with a family—but Picasso considered himself above social rules. He enjoyed Marie-Thérèse's beauty, but his treatment of her, like his treatment of other women, revealed a strong streak of **misogyny.**

In 1928 a Spanish friend taught Picasso to weld. Pablo's interest in sculpture grew, and he produced a series of wire constructions he described as "drawings in space." Picasso's fame was now such that even the **Wall Street Crash** and the beginning of the **Great Depression** in 1929 had no impact on prices for his work. His dealer continued to sell many pieces.

Ever restless, in 1931 Picasso bought a seventeenth-century house outside Paris. He transformed the stables into a sculpture studio. The world celebrated

Marie-Thérèse Walter is shown here with her daughter Maya, Picasso's first daughter, who was born when he was 53 years old.

The Minotaur

In 1933, Picasso launched his own **Surrealist** magazine, *Minotaure*. Picasso had become fascinated with the Greek legend of the Minotaur. In the legend, the Minotaur is a monster, half man, and half bull, that is destroyed by a great hero. To Picasso, the Minotaur represented uncivilized nature, ruled by its own instincts and desires. Picasso saw it as a symbol of his own intense passions and also as a symbol of the beginning of untamed violence in the world. He depicted the violent life of the Minotaur in a large series of etchings and drawings, often portraying Marie-Thérèse as its victim. The rise of the Minotaur in Picasso's work coincided with the rise of **Nazism** in Germany in 1933.

Picasso's 50th birthday with **retrospectives** of his work in Paris and in Zurich, Switzerland. Articles praising his work appeared in newspapers and magazines around the world.

A ruined marriage

Picasso could appear to be a charming, modest, family man. But he could behave like the violent Minotaur he often depicted in his work. He physically and emotionally attacked Olga, and his relationship with Marie-Thérèse became publicly known. By 1935 Picasso's marriage was in ruins. When Olga discovered Marie-Thérèse was pregnant, she finally left, taking fourteen-year-old Paulo with her. Her refusal to grant Picasso a divorce pushed him into another deep depression.

To help him cope, Picasso persuaded his old friend, the Spanish poet Jaime Sabartés, to abandon his family and join him in France. Picasso painted Sabartés as a Spanish **courtier** in a costume. In many ways Sabartés was a courtier to "King" Pablo: the butt of his jokes, and public cheerleader of his master's genius. Until he died, in 1968, Sabartés was Picasso's trusted friend and secretary.

In October 1935, Marie-Thérèse gave birth to Picasso's daughter, Maya. But any new stability in their lives was to be short-lived.

War in Spain

By 1936, Picasso was the most respected artist of the age, and there were major **retrospectives** of his work in Barcelona and Paris. But the lack of privacy, as well as the end of his marriage, drove him from Paris to his vacation home at Juan-Les-Pins with Marie-Thérèse. Despite the collapse of his marriage and the birth of Maya, Picasso treated Marie-Thérèse as an occasional companion rather than a close partner. His great interest at this time was in "found-and-altered" sculpture— taking recognizable objects and combining them with other objects to create completely new forms. He took to gathering junk, including wood, skulls, and beach toys, from the beaches and woods around Juan-Les-Pins. He used this junk as material for his sculptures.

Returning to Paris in July 1936, Picasso learned of the outbreak of the **Spanish Civil War.** The Spanish military and **Fascists,** led by General Franco, had declared war on their democratically elected **Republican** government. Troops and aircraft from **Nazi** Germany and Fascist Italy supported Franco; the Republicans were virtually defenseless. Many sympathetic supporters of the Spanish Republic and democracy—Europeans and Americans—traveled to Spain to fight against Franco.

The influence of Dora Maar

At the same time, Picasso renewed his acquaintance with Dora Maar, a **left-wing** photographer and **Surrealist.** She was as different from Marie-Thérèse as Olga had been from Fernande. Picasso's interest in her was stimulated by her game of driving a penknife quickly between her gloved fingers into the wood of café tables. Whenever she missed and cut herself, blood stained her gloves. Fascinated, Picasso asked for her gloves as mementos. Like the other women in his life, Dora became a source of artistic inspiration for Picasso. Marie-Thérèse, meanwhile, was increasingly ignored and had to endure seeing her image becoming more and more grotesque in Picasso's pictures.

Dora spoke fluent Spanish, so she could discuss the situation in Spain with Picasso in his native language. Influential people in Spain had given speeches doubting Picasso's commitment to the republic, and these led to rumors that he favored the military under Franco. Intense, emotional, and politically committed, Dora encouraged Picasso to express open support for the legitimate Spanish Republican government. When he did, the Spanish government made Picasso honorary director of the national collection of art treasures, at the Prado Museum.

As the civil war continued, Picasso worked on several anti-Fascist and anti-Franco themes, including a series of etchings entitled *The Dream and Lie of Franco*. In these works, his Minotaur image was transformed into a heroic bull. In 1937, Picasso was asked to provide a centerpiece for the Spanish pavilion at the World Fair.

Guernica

Dora helped Picasso find an enormous studio in Paris where he could prepare the work. His initial sketches and ideas were uninspired. Then, on April 26, 1937, the news reported a German bombing raid on a small town in the Basque region of Spain. The town was called Guernica. There were 7,000 people living in Guernica when it was bombed, and about 1,750 people died in the bombing raid. This horrible event gave Picasso a theme.

As Picasso worked on the huge *Guernica* painting, Dora Maar photographed him at work, charting its progress.

Other artists, journalists, photographers, and writers visited him as he worked. In a blizzard of action and inspiration, the 26-foot- (8-meter-) long painting was completed in little over a month. As Picasso worked on the painting, Marie-Thérèse confronted Dora and appealed to Picasso to choose between them. "I like you both," he replied. "You'll have to fight it out yourselves." While the women argued over his affection, Picasso painted on.

Of *Guernica*, Picasso said: "Painting is not done to decorate apartments. It is an instrument of war ... against brutality and darkness." Painted in stark tones of gray, black, charcoal, and white, *Guernica* was inspired by the gruesome war scenes of the Spanish artist **Francisco de Goya,** and photographs of the devastated town that were printed in the French newspaper Ce *Soir.* The mouth of every man, woman, child, horse, and bull screams in pain and terror: the only points of stillness are the corpses of a baby and a soldier.

In addition to *Guernica*, Picasso completed many other canvases that expressed both his feelings of rage and his sense of powerlessness at the violence and the lack of stability in Spain.

In *Guernica*, 1937, Picasso incorporated many of the themes he had used in previous years, including **Cubism, Surrealism,** Greek mythology, and the Minotaur.

> **"** *"In Guernica,"* Picasso said, *"I have clearly expressed my horror of the military caste that has plunged Spain into an ocean of suffering and death."* **"**

As war in Europe approached, *Guernica* traveled the world. It was taken to Norway, then England, and then shipped to the U.S., where it stayed. Meanwhile, Picasso expressed further anguish with the jagged *Weeping Woman* (1937) and a number of violent **still lifes.** He also found a new **metaphor** for the times—a cat playing with a bleeding bird—which he painted again and again. Picasso's paintings of Dora became increasingly vicious and tortured.

The fall of Spain

In 1938, Picasso spent the summer in Mougins, in the south of France. The eventual downfall of the Spanish Republic was already obvious. The Republic could not succeed with Germany and Italy giving so much support to the **Fascists.** Picasso completed several portraits of local people. Many of these paintings have violent themes that express contempt for the world's growing inhumanity. One, *Girl with Cockerel*, shows a young woman about to slaughter a rooster she holds across her lap.

In March 1939, the Republican government finally fell and General Franco made himself **dictator** of Spain. Picasso could no longer return to the land of his birth. Meanwhile, the world paid him more attention. That year the Museum of Modern Art in New York displayed a large Picasso **retrospective.**

Picasso grew more restless. In 1939, he vacationed on the Mediterranean coast. Dora and Marie-Thérèse were amazed to discover he had brought them both with him. From here he traveled to Paris for a funeral but then had his chauffeur drive through the night so he could see a bullfight in Fréjus, France.

On September 1, 1939, it was announced that the German army had invaded Poland. Two days later France declared war on Germany. The violence in Spain would be repeated all over Europe.

World War II

As the **Nazi** leader Hitler prepared to invade Poland, Picasso was in Antibes on the Mediterranean coast, where he painted his last picture in peacetime—*Night Fishing at Antibes*. Then, to escape the political trouble in Paris, Picasso set himself up in a permanent studio in Royan, a town in the French countryside, and traveled regularly between there and Paris.

The war started in earnest in April 1940. Determined not to fight a **trench war** for territory measured in feet, Hitler's generals developed *blitzkrieg*, or lightning war, a tactic of rapid, intense military attack. Helped by the **Allies'** indecision, poor equipment, and incapable leadership, the Germans swept through Western Europe, brushing aside the armies of Belgium, Holland, and France.

Paris in wartime

On June 4, Paris was bombed and *l'exode*, the escape of the civilian population, began. The British Prime Minister Winston Churchill had

Night Fishing at Antibes, 1939, shows Dora Maar and André Breton's wife watching fishermen catch fish by the light of lamps.

German troops entered Paris on June 14, 1940. They occupied the city until 1944.

hoped Paris would be defended district by district. Though many in France shared his wish, French military leaders declared Paris an "open city" and pulled back. Within six weeks the French had signed a humiliating **armistice** with the Germans.

Against the flow of l'exode, Picasso now made his way to Paris, with Sabartés in tow. But he found himself increasingly isolated. Close friends had been forced into **exile,** had been arrested, or were in hiding. Picasso's own freedom of movement was limited by Nazi curfews and travel restrictions. Increasingly Picasso retreated into his studio, which also became his home.

Domestically, Dora and Marie-Thérèse had each decided to pretend that the other did not exist. In 1942, Picasso completed L'Aubade, a somber piece showing two women uncomfortably aware of each other's presence. This was probably based on his home life. That year he also finished a **still life** that captured the severe deprivation of life under German occupation. Pitcher, Candle, and Casserole showed an empty jug and pan, and a candle—the symbol of death.

Picasso's stance of **resistance** to the **Nazis** was one of noble aloofness. While not actively political, he kept his distance from the invaders. He also refused invitations of refuge in other countries. Although his presence in Paris was significant to many French citizens as a sign of resistance to the Nazis, he confided to **Jean Cocteau:** "Everything will go from bad to worse. It's all broken in us."

Recognized in cafés where he went to keep warm, Picasso refused German offers of extra fuel: "A Spaniard is never cold!" Although he was cut off from much of his money, which was kept in banks in other countries, Picasso was very wealthy, but he was still anxious to share the hardships of ordinary French people.

Work in the war years

Picasso's pictures at this time did not show the war directly, but instead reflected the influence of the German occupation through the use of dark, somber colors and gloomy subjects. He also returned to sculpture, mostly using found metal objects.

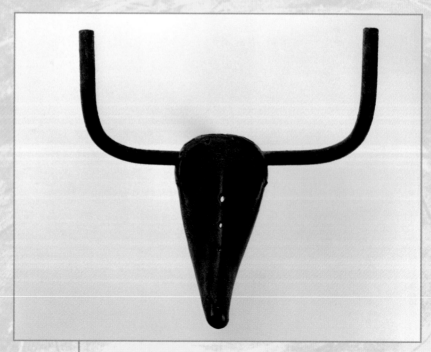

The Bull's Head (1942) is typical of Picasso's "found-and-altered" pieces: "One day I found a bicycle saddle in a pile of old junk, and next to it a rusty set of handle bars. Quick as a flash … the idea of this 'bull's head' came to me."

> **"** **"**
>
> *"I did not paint the war, because I am not one of those artists who go around like photographers to record events. But I have no doubt that the war is contained in the pictures I have painted."*
>
> Picasso explained why the war was not the subject of his work in 1945.

Picasso was criticized by other painters who were **collaborators,** and was forbidden to exhibit his work, but the Germans did not harass him. Although the Nazis labeled him a creator of "degenerate art" they still wanted to buy his canvases. The **Surrealist** painter Oscar Dominguez even made a living selling forged Picassos to Nazis. On one occasion, Picasso distributed postcards of *Guernica* to German officers. One, looking at the picture, asked, "Is this your work?" "No," Picasso replied. "It's yours."

Françoise Gilot

By 1942, Picasso's relationship with Dora was becoming unhappy. In 1943, dining in a Catalán restaurant, he met Françoise Gilot. Tall, slim, and beautiful, she was 20 years younger than Dora and 40 years younger than Picasso, who was now 62. Dora grew increasingly jealous, and although she and Picasso continued to see each other until 1946, separation was inevitable. In one confrontation, she accused Picasso: "You've never loved anyone in your life. You don't know how to love." Eventually Dora had a nervous breakdown and left Picasso. She rebuilt her life by becoming active in painting and photography in the Provence area of France.

When Paris was liberated from the Nazis in August 1944, thousands of friends and well-wishers visited Picasso. In October, Picasso's work was the subject of a special exhibition at the Salon in Paris, an annual French exhibition of contemporary art. Until this point, Picasso had never taken part in the Salon.

Picasso's response to war is seen in his art before and after Hitler's war, rather than during it. Following the liberation of Paris, Picasso prepared one of his most important war paintings. He was also about to drop his own political bombshell.

Creating the Picasso Legend

In late 1944, Picasso announced that he had joined the French **Communist** Party. There was a great outcry from some—and celebration from others. He was personally encouraged by his friend, the **Surrealist** poet **Paul Éluard,** but he was also attracted by the heroic role Communist Party members had played in the **resistance** movement and the popular respect they commanded after the liberation. "Were the Communists not the most courageous people in France?" he asked. "Until the day when Spain can welcome me back, the French Communist Party [has] opened its arms to me and I found in it those that I most value, the greatest scientists, the greatest poets, all those beautiful faces of Parisian insurgents ... I am once more among my brothers."

Éluard also introduced Picasso to Pierre Daix, a Communist recently liberated from a **Nazi concentration camp.** Daix told Picasso how the thought of *Guernica* had helped him during his years in the camp. Daix later became a close friend and a devoted cataloger of Picasso's work, and Picasso made contributions to a magazine edited by Daix.

Political paintings

Several of Picasso's paintings of this period have a clear political content, though the number of actively political works in his total output was minimal. *The Charnel House* was inspired by the shocking accounts about life in the Nazi concentration camps that were starting to appear in the press.

In 1951, Picasso completed *Massacre in Korea*, a painting about the Korean War based on execution scenes in paintings by **Goya** and **Manet.** However, many senior Communist Party officials condemned it for not going far enough in rebuking the Americans for their actions. In 1953 the Soviet **dictator** Joseph Stalin died, and Picasso was asked to do a portrait for the French Communist Party newspaper. His picture caused a scandal in the Communist Party for not being realistic, and Picasso was severely criticized, although Daix supported his painting.

The Charnel House, 1945, features a pile of hideously broken bodies, reflecting scenes from Nazi concentration camps.

Paintings of celebration

Other paintings celebrated the dawn of a new age and the joy of the living. *Joie de Vivre,* or *Joy of Life,* and *Faun Piping* recalled a mythical ancient Greece populated by fictional animals, heroes, and gods. By now the myth of Picasso itself was taking over. According to Timothy Hilton, "the works of art that he produced for the next 20 years ... are interesting primarily because it was Picasso who produced them."

New directions

Picasso's personal life was as complicated as ever. In 1945, he took his new partner, Françoise Gilot, to his house in Ménerbes, France. He was also in daily correspondence with Marie-Thérèse until 1946, when he ended his relationship with her and returned to Antibes with Françoise.

In 1947, following the birth of their son Claude, Picasso and Françoise moved into a house called La Galloise in Vallauris, France. He could afford luxury, but Picasso seemed not to care about the primitive conditions of the house and the basic sanitation.

Picasso is shown here with Françoise Gilot and their son, Claude, at Vallauris. When Françoise left Picasso, he refused to see their children.

The little town, largely **Communist,** had once been a center of pottery making, but the industry was in decline. Picasso rescued the ceramics trade in Vallauris with a period of furious production, creating 2,000 pieces of pottery in one year. The pieces were quirky—animal-shaped drinking vessels and jugs,—and were made with red-brown clay finished in brown and white paint. Local craftsmen produced large quantities of the ceramic pieces he had designed, to meet the enormous demand for his work.

> "Everything Picasso touched underwent a vital transformation. He brought renewed prosperity to the place he lived and new prestige to the medium in which he worked."
>
> In 1993, James Lord, an art historian, described the Picasso legend.

Mounted Rider, 1951, a ceramic wine pitcher, was one of the many playful ceramic pieces that Picasso completed in Vallauris.

New techniques

For several years, Picasso also experimented with **lithography,** a printing technique that uses ink and a smooth surface to create images. In 1949, his lithograph *Dove of Peace* was adopted as the emblem of the International Peace Congress. That same year, he and Françoise had a daughter, Paloma—Spanish for "dove." After the war, the revival of bullfighting in southern France rekindled Picasso's enthusiasm for the spectacle. In the 1950s he created a series of lithographs called *La Tauromaquia,* or *The Bullfight*.

Picasso took special pleasure in painting his young children at play, reading, or lying asleep. The children's toys also inspired several sculptures. For one of these sculptures, Picasso created the head of a baboon out of one of Claude's toy cars.

49

In 1952, Picasso created his *Temple de la Paix*, or *Temple of Peace*, in a ruined chapel in Vallauris. This contained his *War and Peace* murals, a clearly political effort that received much attention from the world's media, raising Picasso's public profile still further.

Françoise leaves

Picasso was constantly in the public eye. Relaxing on the beach he would amuse himself by doodling in the sand, to the fascination of bystanders, and play with his children, pretending not to notice onlookers. But cracks were appearing in his relationship with Françoise. She did not enjoy the unwanted attention of strangers on the beach, or the uninvited guests who would appear at La Galloise. Three years later she left Picasso, which shamed and angered him. As **Cocteau** wrote to a friend: "Picasso likes to do the leaving, not to be left."

Gilot's memoirs showed Picasso's character in a poor light. She told readers that he was a genius of electrifying talent, but also a cruel man with a ferocious ego. She described his cruelty to women and his immature behavior. Picasso tried to keep Gilot from publishing the book, but the courts decided she had the legal right to publish it. Furious, Picasso refused to see Gilot or their children, Claude and Paloma, again. He did not acknowledge their existence.

Jacqueline Roque

For Picasso, 1953–54 was a period of self-critical despair, resulting in gloomy and introspective work. In 1954, however, he began a relationship with Jacqueline Roque. His work returned to more outward-looking themes.

Picasso enjoyed his celebrity status, but his fame forced him to leave his homes in Paris and Vallauris. Picasso was so rich he could lock up one home and move to another, leaving everything—furniture, canvases, and collections of junk—in place.

Picasso and Jacqueline moved to a home near Cannes, France that they called La Californie. Picasso worked in the large pigeon loft, often painting the sea view from the window. When his great rival **Matisse**

died in 1954, Picasso completed a series of variations on *The Women of Algiers*, by **Delacroix**—one of Matisse's idols—in his honor. He publicly acclaimed his regard for his rival's originality and greatness: "All things considered," Picasso said, "there's only Matisse."

In retreat

The bustle and noise of Cannes became oppressive and Picasso and Jacqueline moved to the peace and quiet of a house called Vauvenargues, near the small French town Aix-en-Provence. The frequent moves from house to house in the middle of the 1950s were part of Picasso's gradual retreat from public life. Despite his age and his increasing isolation Picasso showed no sign of retiring. He continued to work on his art every day.

51

Some writers called the paintings Picasso completed in Vauvenargues his Spanish Period. During these years, his ties with Spain—a land he had not seen since the 1930s—grew stronger. Spanish visitors told him how popular his work was in his native land. Picasso also published three poems in Spanish.

Olga had died in 1955, so in 1961 Picasso was able to marry Jacqueline. They moved to another new home, Villa Notre-Dame-de-Vie at Mougins. Although he celebrated his 80th birthday with feasting, an exhibition of his work, and a bullfight, Picasso lived and worked in relative seclusion at Notre-Dame-de-Vie.

Picasso renewed his interest in sculpture in the early 1960s, cutting and bending huge figures from sheet metal, which he then painted, and sandblasting sculptures from concrete. He also devoted considerable energy to engravings.

The last years

Picasso always drew inspiration from many sources —his artistic contemporaries, the **old masters, primitive art,** myths, and legends. He was at the forefront of modern art, but he often looked to the past and the works of highly respected **Renaissance** artists. In conversations, he frequently ranked himself alongside them rather than his young contemporaries. But many people maintain that the quality of his work from 1945 onward was poor. One art historian said *Massacre in Korea* was so bad it was

In the 1960s, Picasso renewed his interest in sculpture. *Football Player*, 1965, demonstrates his playful sense of humor as well as his acute artistic eye.

embarrassing. Despite the poor quality of some of his late pieces, the quantity of his work increased right up to his death. In his eighties Picasso would complete between three and five paintings a day, sometimes working on several at the same time. Although Picasso's late work was variously described as "the incoherent scribblings of a[n] ... old man," and the work of "the most youthful artist alive," his need to express himself through art kept him working.

Picasso returned to a favorite theme—the artist's relationship with his model. But now his model, Jacqueline, was also his caretaker. Picasso hated being physically dependent on her and he sometimes treated her very cruelly as a result. Some of Picasso's final work echoed with the faint images of the African masks that had startled and influenced him in the Trocadéro Museum many years before. "I must find the mask," he said.

This photograph of Picasso and Jacqueline was taken in 1961. In old age, Picasso became increasingly dependent on Jacqueline's support.

To mark Picasso's 85th birthday, the French government organized an international exhibition of 500 works. At 90 years old, he became the first painter to be given a one-man show at the Louvre in the artist's own lifetime.

Pablo Picasso died on April 8, 1973 at his home in Mougins. He was 91 years old. The estimated value of his estate was over $80 million. Jacqueline Picasso devoted herself to caring for his artistic legacy, just as she had cared for him, until her death in 1986.

Picasso's Legacy

Pablo Picasso was the first truly world-famous artist in the age of mass media. Like the half man, half bull Minotaur, he tore through the world of art to put himself at the forefront of the **Modernist** revolution. The unstoppable Picasso helped create widespread artistic awareness and defined the popular image of the artist.

Picasso had a huge influence on artists. As the British sculptor Henry Moore said: "Picasso and the British Museum were the only inspiration I needed." But writers, photographers, journalists, poets, and philosophers were also charmed by and interested in this energetically creative man.

He completed thousands of paintings, etchings, ceramics, and sculptures. In his Blue and Rose Periods he created some of the most haunting images ever painted. **Cubism** became one of the most influential artistic movements of the twentieth century. It was a major change in the way artists thought about painting. Painting was no longer a representation of how the world was, but an expression of what the artist thought about it. Cubism inspired all different kinds of artists, on many levels: from sculpture to literature, from poetry to fashion and ceramic design. Picasso was a major inspiration for the **Surrealists.** Paintings such as *Guernica*, and Picasso's later political associations again showed the political role artists can play in society.

Picasso flirted with the media to promote his art. When being photographed working on *Guernica* or filmed in Vallauris, Picasso made himself as important as his art, and carefully created the enduring myth of Picasso.

Many artists who followed him—Andy Warhol and Jackson Pollock, to name a few—are famous for their celebrated but controversial artistic styles. But none became as recognizable in so many different styles as Picasso. As the art historian Timothy Hilton said, many artists based their entire careers on what Picasso might have invented and played with for a year or two before moving on to something completely new.

In 1948 Picasso posed at Vallauris, painting a ceramic bowl. He was always aware of the importance of the role of the media in keeping the "Picasso myth" going.

Some people accuse Picasso of stealing ideas. In working with contemporaries in Paris, such as **Braque,** he would naturally have exchanged ideas and found influences. He was also fiercely competitive, sometimes to the point of being cruel, and was quick to diminish the artists who shared their ideas with him. But Picasso combined his unique perspective and vision with outside influences to create new and totally original art.

As a man, Picasso had deep faults. He was a self-centered bully, and his treatment of his friends and of the women and children in his life was appalling. Few of his companions escaped Picasso's life with their spirits intact: many suffered mental illness, and his treatment of Eva may have accelerated her death. His verbal and physical abuse of others may have been a way of hiding deep insecurities about himself.

Throughout his life, Picasso portrayed his subjects in masks, including the mask of the clown, and primitive masks. At the end of his life he still hunted "the mask." Perhaps the reason Picasso was so interested in masks is that he hid his true, insecure self behind the image of a happy, confident artist for his entire life.

55

Timeline

1881	Pablo Ruiz y Picasso is born on October 25 in Málaga, in Spain.
1888	Picasso's father starts to teach him how to paint.
1892	Picasso enters art school at La Coruña.
1895	Picasso moves to Barcelona and enters the School of Fine Arts.
1897	*Science and Charity* is painted. Picasso attends the Royal Academy, in Madrid.
1899	Picasso meets the artistic **avant-garde** in Barcelona.
1900	Picasso visits Paris; shares a studio with friend and fellow artist Casagemas, and agrees to sell all his paintings to Petrus Mañach.
1901	*Yo Picasso* and *Child Holding a Dove* are painted. Casagemas commits suicide in Paris; Picasso's Blue Period begins. *Evocation (The Burial of Casagemas)* is painted.
1904	Picasso settles in Paris, and moves to the *Bateau Lavoir.* Picasso meets Fernande Olivier, who becomes his companion until 1911. *Woman with a Crow* and *Woman Ironing* are painted.
1905	Picasso's Rose Period begins, and he paints *Family of Acrobats with an Ape*, *Boy with a Pipe*, and *At the Lapin Agile.*
1906	*Self-Portrait with Palette* and *Portrait of Gertrude Stein* are painted.
1907	Picasso paints *Les Demoiselles d'Avignon* but immediately hides it, and it is not seen in public for many years. Picasso meets **Georges Braque,** and they develop **Cubism.** Picasso paints *The Dryad* (1908), *The Reservoir at Horta De Ebro* (1909), *Violin and Grapes* (1912), and *Ma Jolie* (1914).
1912–13	Picasso makes *Guitar*. This introduces a new form of sculpture.
1913	Picasso's father dies, and Picasso, Braque, and **Gris** develop **Synthetic Cubism.**
1917	Picasso designs costumes and sets for the ballet *Parade*, and meets the dancer Olga Koklova. Picasso's sketches include a portrait of Stravinsky.
1918	Olga and Picasso are married.

1920	Picasso paints *Still Life on a Table*.
1921	Olga and Picasso's son Paulo is born.
	Three Musicians, and *Mother and Child* are painted in 1921. Picasso also paints *Women Running on the Beach (The Race)* (1922), *Paulo Drawing* (1923), and *Portrait of Olga* (1923)
1925	Picasso takes part in the first **Surrealist** exhibition. *Les Demoiselles d'Avignon* is reproduced for the first time. Picasso paints *The Three Dancers*.
1927	Picasso meets Marie-Thérèse Walter.
1928–31	Picasso sculpts *Wire Constructions* (1928–29). Picasso's Surrealist painting phase includes *Seated Bather* (1930), and *Figures by the Sea (The Kiss)* (1931).
1935	Marie-Thérèse and Picasso's daughter Maya is born.
1936	The **Spanish Civil War** begins. **Retrospectives** of Picasso's career are held in Barcelona, Madrid, Paris, and London. Picasso begins a relationship with photographer Dora Maar.
1937	Picasso paints *Guernica*, *Weeping Woman*, and *Portrait of Dora Maar*.
1939	Picasso paints *Cat Devouring a Bird* and *Night Fishing at Antibes*. World War II begins.
1940–44	Picasso spends the war years in occupied Paris.
1942	Picasso sculpts *Bull's Head*.
1944	Picasso joins the **Communist** Party of France.
1945	Picasso begins a relationship with Françoise Gilot. Picasso paints *The Charnel House*.
1947	Picasso and Françoise settle in Vallauris, and their son Claude is born.
1949	Picasso and Françoise's daughter Paloma is born.
1953	Françoise leaves Picasso.
1954	Picasso begins a relationship with Jacqueline Roque, and paints *Jacqueline Roque with Flowers*.
1961	Picasso marries Jacqueline Roque, and becomes more reclusive.
1973	Picasso dies on April 8, in Mougins, from complications caused by influenza.

Picasso's Friends and Influences

Apollinaire, Guillaume (1880–1918) French poet, writer, and art critic; leader of a Parisian movement rejecting traditional rules of poetry

Braque, Georges (1882–1963) French painter who developed Cubism with Picasso

Breton, André (1896–1966) Radical French poet and writer, and founding member of the Surrealist movement who joined the Communist Party in 1930

Cézanne, Paul (1839–1906) French Post-Impressionist painter and forerunner of Cubism

Chanel, Gabrielle "Coco" (1883–1971) French fashion designer, perfumer, and jeweler

Cocteau, Jean (1889–1963) French poet, playwright, artist, and filmmaker, who sponsored Picasso, Stravinsky, Diaghilev, and the Ballets Russes

Degas, Edgar (1834–1917) French painter who worked with the Impressionists, painting scenes of modern life, including ballet dancers, café society, and laundry women

Delacroix, Eugène (1798–1863) French painter and leader of the Romantic Movement who used bright colors and influenced Matisse

Derain, André (1880–1954) French painter, theater designer, and book illustrator who was closely associated with Matisse

Diaghilev, Serge (1872–1929) Russian ballet manager who worked with some of Europe's greatest names in music, art, and dance

Éluard, Paul (1895–1952) French poet and founder of the Surrealist movement in literature

Goya, Francisco de (1746–1828) Spanish painter in the court of King Charles IV whose works include *The Disasters of War*, depicting the horrors committed during Napoleon's invasion of Spain

Greco, El (1541–1614) Nickname of Domenikos Theotokopoulos, a Greek artist who settled in Spain and became a portrait painter

Gris, Juan (1887–1927) Pseudonym of José Victoriano González, a Spanish-born painter who developed Synthetic Cubism

Jacob, Max (1876–1944) Poet and writer, and one of the first French artists to befriend and promote the talent of young Picasso

Laurencin, Marie (1885–1956) French painter and print-maker influenced by Matisse, Cézanne, Gauguin, and the cubists

Manet, Édouard (1832–1883) French painter who painted modern life in the style of the old masters, and was associated with the Impressionists and Post-Impressionists

Matisse, Henri (1869–1954) French artist famous for his vivid use of primary colors, influenced by Cubism and Impressionism

Miró, Joan (1893–1983) Spanish Surrealist and abstract artist

Monet, Claude (1840–1926) French Impressionist artist

Pissarro, Camille (1830–1903) French Impressionist artist

Raphael (1483–1520) Italian painter who painted during the Renaissance

Renoir, Pierre-Auguste (1841–1919) French Impressionist artist

Stein, Gertrude (1874–1946) American-born writer who settled in Paris and involved herself in the world of experimental art and writing

Toulouse-Lautrec, Henri (1864–1901) French painter and printmaker who painted dancers, cabaret acts, actors, circus performers, and bar staff

Glossary

Allies countries that fought against Germany in World War II, including England, France, Australia, the U.S., and the Soviet Union

Anarchism political theory that claims that any organized government system is oppressive

armistice peace treaty signaling the end of a conflict

automatism Surrealist technique of painting or writing by "emptying the mind" and letting the pen be guided by the subconscious

avant-garde describes a pioneer or innovator in the arts

bohemian socially different, free-and-easy person; term especially used to describe artists and writers

classical art of ancient Greece or Rome, or art in that style

collaborator person who actively aids or otherwise helps the enemy

Communist believer in a political idea that has at its heart the idea of equality for all, and common ownership of all property; associated with the writings of Karl Marx and the 1917 revolution in Russia

concentration camp kind of camp used extensively by the Nazis where political opponents, racial minorities, and others were sent to do hard labor or be put to death

courtier person who serves the king or queen in a court

Cubism attempt to show all four dimensions—height, width, depth, and time—in a two- or three-dimensional art form. Cubism allowed the examination of an object from a variety of viewpoints, rather than the single viewpoint of traditional painting.

curator keeper of a museum or art collection

dictator leader of a country who rules with unrestricted authority. Franco (of Spain) and Hitler (of Germany) were dictators.

diphtheria once common and often fatal infection of the throat and larynx

dyslexia disorder in which a person finds it hard to read numbers and letters correctly

elitist person who believes that a select group of people is better than other groups

exile being forced to leave a country and go live elsewhere, usually because of political beliefs

Fascist supporter of Fascism, a form of extreme dictatorship, characterized by aggressive Nationalism and anti-Communism

Great Depression worldwide economic collapse that followed the Wall Street Crash and contributed to the rise of Nazism in Europe and World War II

hypochondria mental condition that makes people obsessed with their health, resulting in them thinking they are ill whether they are or not

hypocrisy act of doing something that you do not agree with so that you will look good

Impressionism artistic movement in France around the 1860s, which rejected the dark colors of studio painting and tried to capture the brilliant effects of sunlight, shadow, water, and fog. Painters who painted in this style are called Impressionists.

Jazz Age period of wealth, freedom, and pleasure between the end of World War I and the beginning of the Great Depression

left-wing describes someone with Socialist political views

lithography printing process that places an image on a smooth surface and rubs ink on it to make multiple copies

metaphor word or image in language or art where an idea or being is represented by something else

middle class group of people between the working class and the rich

misogyny hatred of women

Modernism term used to describe the bold experiments in artistic activity during the early part of the twentieth century

monarchy political system based on kingship and hereditary rule

Nationalist person who believes in the liberation of their country from an invader or foreign rulers, or someone who puts the interest of their nation and national group above all else, turning against outsiders, foreigners, and minorities

Nazism term which comes from the National Socialist German Workers' Party, a political party founded in 1919, and led by Adolf Hitler. Nazis believed in Nationalism, racism, and the power of the state over the individual.

old masters collective name given to the great artists who created art before 1750

primitive art art and sculpture of the pre-conquest peoples of Latin America, Africa, and the Pacific, and the prehistoric peoples of Europe

Renaissance term used to describe the period of great discoveries in learning and art which took place in Europe, and especially Italy, in the fourteenth, fifteenth, and sixteenth centuries

Republican follower of a system of government that relies on elected heads of state

resistance name given to all forms of opposition to the German occupation in World War II

retrospective exhibition looking back at the work of a particular artist to show how their work developed over their lifetime

Socialism political theory that believes in a more equal distribution of income and resources, and in government direction and control of all economic activity

Spanish Civil War war between the Spanish army, aided by Fascist Italy and Nazi Germany, and the elected Republican government in 1936. The Spanish army won, and Franco became dictator of Spain.

still life painting of an arrangement of one or several inanimate objects, such as fruit, flowers, vases, and musical instruments

subconscious thought or feeling in a person's mind that the person is not fully aware of

Surrealism artistic movement outlined in 1924 by André Breton, based on the absurd, heightened and distorted reality, dreams, and the work of the psychiatrist Sigmund Freud

symbolism use of symbols, sculptures, or objects to stand for something else, usually an idea that is hard to illustrate

Synthetic Cubism development of Cubism, involving larger, more understandable abstract forms and colors, and creating shapes that were recognizable as familiar objects, such as a guitar. Collage was also part of this movement.

trench war war fought between armies from fixed positions and fortifications, usually dug in the ground

tuberculosis also known as TB; a serious, once fatal, lung infection

Wall Street Crash collapse of prices on the New York Stock Exchange in October 1929, which led to the Great Depression, a worldwide economic collapse

Places to Visit

Art Institute of Chicago
111 South Michigan Ave.
Chicago, IL 60603
312-443-3600

Los Angeles County Museum of Art
5905 Wiltshire Blvd.
Los Angeles, CA 90036
323-857-6000

Museum of Fine Art, Boston
465 Huntington Ave.
Boston, MA 02115
617-267-9300

National Gallery of Art
Sixth St. and Constitution Ave.
Washington, D.C. 20565
202-737-4215

San Francisco Museum of Modern Art
151 Third Street
San Francisco, CA 94103
415-357-4000

Cleveland Museum of Art
11150 East Boulevard
University Circle
Cleveland, OH 44106
216-421-7340

Metropolitan Museum of Art
1000 Fifth Avenue
New York, NY 10028
212-535-7710

Museum of Modern Art
11 W. 53rd Street
New York, NY 10019
212-708-9400

Portland Art Museum
1219 S.W. Park Ave.
Portland, OR 97205
503-226-2811

More Books to Read

Glubock, Shirley. *The Young Picasso*. New York: Simon and Schuster Children's Publishing, 2001.

Picasso, Pablo. *Picasso: Painter and Sculptor in Clay*. New York: Harry N. Abrams, Inc., 1999.

Selfridge, John W. *Pablo Picasso*. Broomall, Pa.: Chelsea House Publishers, 1994.

Index